THE BOYS THAT VANISHED

The Missing Boys' Story"

JOHNSON DOLLAR

Copyright © 2024

JOHNSON DOLLAR

Table of Contents

Johnson Dollar

THE BOYS THAT VANISHED

The Missing Boys' Story "

INTRODUCTION

Once upon a time in the picturesque town of Everwood there were three inseparable friends: Oliver, Max and Ethan. They were known throughout the city for their mischievous adventures and unbreakable bond. One sunny afternoon, while exploring the forest on the outskirts of town, they came across an ancient oak tree with strange symbols carved into its trunk.

Intrigued, the boys approached the tree and ran their hands over the mysterious symbols. Suddenly, a blinding light engulfed them, and when it faded, they found themselves in a strange realm unlike anything they had ever seen.

The boys soon realized that they had been transported to a magical land known as Varinthia, a place where time stood still and dreams came true. Excited but wary, they set out on a journey to uncover the secrets of this enchanting world.

While exploring Varinthia, they encountered mythical creatures, enchanted forests, and hidden treasures beyond their wildest imaginations. Each day brought new adventures and challenges, strengthening their friendship and molding them into brave and resourceful young men.

However, as time passed, the boys began to notice strange changes in themselves. Their laughter became less loud, their voices weakened, and their once vibrant personalities began to fade. Concerned, they sought the guidance of a wise elder of Varinthia who revealed the truth of their predicament.

The elder explained that Varinthia was a realm fueled by the dreams and desires of those who entered it. However, as the boys were consumed by the wonders of this world, they unknowingly began to lose touch with their own reality. Their souls were slowly absorbed by Varinthia, leaving behind only empty shells of their former selves.

Determined to break free from Varinthia's grasp, the boys embark on a perilous quest to find the fabled Fountain of Dreams, the only source of power capable of restoring their lost souls. On their journey, they faced countless obstacles and trials, testing their courage and determination like never before.

After many trials and tribulations, the boys finally reached the Fountain of Dreams. With shaking hands, they dipped their fingers into the shimmering waters and felt a rush of energy coursing through their veins. As the last rays of the sun kissed the horizon, they closed their eyes and made a wish with all their hearts.

In an instant they were back under an ancient oak tree in the Everwood, the markings on its trunk glowing softly in the gloom. With tears of joy streaming down their faces, they hugged each other tightly, grateful to be together again.

From that day on, Oliver, Max, and Ethan cherished every moment together, knowing that their bond was stronger than any magic the world could offer. And even though their adventure in Varinthia is over, the memories they shared will remain in their hearts forever.

In the field of art, history whispers secrets and every brushstroke tells a story. Among the countless stories that adorn the annals of artistic endeavor, there is a captivating saga known as "The Boys That Varnished." This mysterious story combines elements of talent, ambition and relentless pursuit of creative expression, leaving an indelible mark on the canvas of art history.

Imagine being transported to the bustling streets of 19th century Paris, where the air is saturated with the scent of colors and the promise of an artistic revolution. It is in this vibrant environment that our story takes place, centered around a group of young, daring artists who have dared to defy convention and challenge the status quo.

At its heart, The Boys That Varnished is a chronicle of camaraderie and artistic camaraderie that transcends time and tradition. United by a common passion for innovation and a desire for recognition, these young visionaries embarked on a journey full of triumphs and tribulations.

Fueled by their unwavering determination, the boys set out to revolutionize the art world, armed with nothing but their brushes and boundless creativity. It was a quest for artistic immortality, a tireless pursuit of perfection that knew no bounds.

But what sets this story apart from the countless others that have preceded it? It's an element of mystery that shrouds the identity of these intrepid artists and casts a veil of intrigue over their actions. Who were these enigmatic figures who dared to challenge the conventions of their time? What made them defy the established norms of the art world and forge their own path?

As we delve deeper into the annals of history, we uncover tantalizing clues that offer glimpses into the lives of these elusive artists. It is a story of victory over adversity, of perseverance in the face of insurmountable obstacles. It is a testament to the power of artistic expression to overcome barriers and connect souls across generations.

Join me as we embark on a journey of discovery, peeling back the layers of time to uncover the hidden truths behind "The Boys That Varnished." Together we will unravel the mysteries that have shrouded their legacy for centuries and shed new light on their extraordinary contribution to the world of art.

Ultimately, "The Boys That Varnished" stands as a testament to the enduring power of creativity and the timeless appeal of artistic expression. Their legacy, which continues to inspire and captivate, reminds us that true greatness knows no bounds.

Chapter 1: The Mysterious Disappearance

In the peaceful town of Everwood, among ancient forests and meandering rivers, the sense of tranquility was at odds with the hidden mysteries that seemed to permeate the very essence of the land. For generations, the city's cobbled streets have been filled with whispers, stories of unexplained events and disappearing souls that have left an indelible mark on the collective consciousness of its inhabitants. None of these legends intrigued as much as the story of the missing boys - a trio of friends whose fates became intertwined with the mysterious aura of Everwood.

Oliver, Max and Ethan were inseparable companions, their laughter echoing through the woods as they explored every nook and cranny of their idyllic hometown. Their bond was forged in the fire of childhood friendship, unbreakable and pure. But one fateful autumn evening, as the sun sank below the horizon and cast long shadows over the sleepy town, three friends embarked on an adventure that would change the course of their lives forever.

It started innocently enough, courage whispered between friends under the shady canopy of the forest. Drawn by curiosity and youthful exuberance, Oliver suggested they venture deep into the woods, where rumors of strange happenings and hidden treasures abounded. Eager to prove their bravery, Max and Ethan readily agreed, their hearts pounding with excitement as they plunged into the darkness that lay beyond the safety of their familiar surroundings.

As they made their way through the labyrinthine maze of trees and undergrowth, the air was thick with an otherworldly calm and a sense of unease crept into the boys' hearts. Still, fueled by adrenaline and the promise of adventure, they pressed on, their footsteps softly crunching against the forest floor.

Hours passed and they still found no trace of the elusive secrets they sought. The forest seemed to stretch endlessly, its secrets guarded by an unseen force that defied their efforts to reveal them. Exhausted and disoriented, the boys came upon a clearing bathed in moonlight, its eerie stillness casting a spell of confusion over their senses.

That's when they saw it, a towering monolith of stone rising from the ground like a silent guardian of the ancient ages. Its weathered surface was decorated with intricately carved symbols, the meaning of which has been lost in the chronicles of time. Inexplicably drawn to the ancient artifact, the boys approached with trepidation, their hands shaking as they reached out to touch its roughly hewn surface.

At that moment, a sudden gust of wind swept through the clearing, carrying with it a haunting melody that seemed to emanate from the very depths of the earth. The ground beneath their feet trembled, and before they could react, a blinding flash of light engulfed them, engulfing them whole, leaving behind nothing but a whisper in the wind.

As dawn broke and the townspeople awoke to find their beloved sons gone, panic spread like wildfire through the streets of Everwood. Search parties were organized and every corner of the forest was searched in a desperate attempt to find any trace of the lost boys. But as days turned to weeks and weeks to months, hope began to fade and the town came to terms with the grim reality of their fate.

Yet even in the depths of despair, whispers lingered among the townspeople, whispers of ancient legends and forgotten truths that spoke of the darkness lurking at the heart of Everwood. And while the fate of Oliver, Max and Ethan remained shrouded in mystery, their disappearance served as a haunting reminder of the unseen forces that controlled their world.

For in the city of Everwood, where shadows danced on the edge of perception and secrets lay buried beneath the soil, the truth was never far away, if only one dared to seek it. And so the story of the missing boys lived on, a cautionary tale for those who dared to tread where others feared to roam.

1.1 Introduction to the protagonists and their Everwood small-town life.

Nestled between rolling green hills and whispering pines, life unfolds at a leisurely pace in the quaint and picturesque town of Everwood, where time seems to stand still and a close-knit community thrives. At the heart of this idyllic setting are three young protagonists whose lives intertwine amidst the rustic charm and simple pleasures of small-town life: Oliver, Max and Ethan.

With his tousled hair and serious blue eyes, Oliver is the epitome of the quintessential small town boy. Born and raised in Everwood, he knows every street corner, every hidden path, and every secret place where wildflowers abound. Despite his carefree demeanor, Oliver harbors dreams of exploration and adventure beyond his familiar surroundings. His restless spirit longs for something more, yet remains rooted in the timeless traditions and values of his beloved hometown.

On the other hand, Max is the new kid on the block who recently moved with his family to Everwood in search of a fresh start. With his urban slicker clothes and air of mystery, Max stands out among the familiar faces of the town and arouses the curiosity and skepticism of the locals. Despite his initial misgivings, Max soon finds himself enchanted by the rustic charm of Everwood and captivated by its warm and welcoming community. As Max navigates the ups and downs of his new life, he discovers unexpected friendships and hidden talents he never knew he possessed.

Ethan completes the trio of main characters, a quiet and introspective soul with a love of nature running deep in his veins. As the son of the local Everwood Park Ranger, Ethan has spent his entire life surrounded by the breathtaking beauty of the wilderness, finding solace and refuge in its embrace. With his keen eye for detail and unwavering determination, Ethan serves as a voice of reason among his friends, offering wise counsel and gentle encouragement whenever they find themselves at a crossroads.

Together, Oliver, Max, and Ethan go through the trials and tribulations of adolescence, forming a bond that transcends time and space. From carefree days spent fishing by the river to moonlit nights under a canopy of stars, their adventures in Everwood are filled with laughter, tears and moments of deep self-discovery. Yet beneath the surface of their seemingly idyllic existence, a shadow looms on the horizon that threatens to shatter the tranquility of their small-town paradise.

Unbeknownst to the people of Everwood, a group of mysterious boys have descended upon the town, their intentions shrouded in mystery and their presence causing whispers of concern among the townspeople. With their mysterious leader and quiet demeanor, these boys seem to materialize out of thin air, leaving a trail of confusion and chaos in their wake. When Oliver, Max, and Ethan find themselves drawn into an unfolding mystery, they must face their deepest fears and uncover the truth before it's too late.

In the timeless tapestry of small-town life in Everwood, where every cobblestone has a story and every whisper holds a secret, the fates of Oliver, Max and Ethan are intricately intertwined, bound by bonds of friendship and enduring spirit. adventure. As they embark on a journey of self-discovery and exploration, they realize that the true magic of Everwood lies not in its peaceful landscape or strange traditions, but in the unbreakable bonds of love and friendship that endure long after the last page. He turned around.

1.2 The sudden disappearance of three boys from the neighborhood.

In the heart of Everwood, a quaint and tight-knit neighborhood where laughter once filled the air, an unsettling aura now looms. The sudden disappearance of three young boys has cast a shadow over the community and left residents grappling with fear and uncertainty. As the days stretch into weeks, speculation swirls and rumors multiply, but answers remain elusive.

It was an ordinary afternoon when the boys, best friends since kindergarten, went to the forest behind their homes. Their laughter echoed through the trees as they embarked on their usual adventure, oblivious to the ominous turn fate would take. Hours passed and when it got dark the boys couldn't get home. Panic gripped the neighborhood as a frantic search yielded no trace of the missing trio.

As word of the disappearance spread, Everwood turned into a hive of activity. Volunteers combed the thick foliage, law enforcement launched a wide-ranging investigation, and concerned residents rallied in solidarity. But despite their tireless efforts, the boys seemed to disappear without a trace, leaving behind a void that was reflected in unanswered questions.

For the families of the missing boys, each passing day is an agonizing ordeal filled with anxiety and despair. Every unopened door, every unanswered phone call serves as a cruel reminder of their absence. They spend sleepless nights clinging to hope, desperate for any sign of where their beloved children are.

As the investigation progresses, theories emerge, each more chilling than the last. Some whispers of foul play hint that sinister forces lurk in the shadows of Everwood. Others point to the woods themselves, a labyrinth of mystery and danger where anything can hide. And then there are those who cling to hope and refuse to believe that their boys will never return.

In the midst of uncertainty, a once-vibrant neighborhood now stands shrouded in sadness. Playgrounds lie deserted, laughter replaced by solemn silence as families grapple with the harsh reality of their new normal. But amidst the darkness, there are glimmers of light as the community gathers in solidarity, united in their search for answers.

As days turn into weeks, the search for the missing boys continues unabated. With each sunrise, hope is rekindled, fueling the determination of those who refuse to give in to despair. The heart of Everwood may be heavy with sadness, but beneath the surface lies a resilience that refuses to be extinguished.

The sudden disappearance of the three boys left an indelible mark on Everwood, a scar that may never fully heal. But as the community stands united in their resolve, they cling to the belief that one day their boys will return home and the laughter that once filled the air will once again echo through the streets. Until then, they wait with bated breath and pray for a miracle that will bring their children back into their loving arms.

1.3 Initial investigations by local authorities and the community's shock.

Everwood, a picturesque town surrounded by lush forests and peaceful countryside, has been thrown into a state of shock and disbelief after the sudden and mysterious disappearance of three young boys: Oliver, Max and Ethan. As local authorities begin an initial investigation, a tight-knit community grapples with fear and uncertainty as they try to make sense of the mysterious circumstances surrounding the disappearance of these beloved children.

The unfolding of events began one seemingly ordinary evening as Oliver, Max and Ethan ventured into the woods on the edge of Everwood, their laughter echoing through the peaceful air as they embarked on what was supposed to be a routine adventure. But when night fell and the boys did not return home, panic set in among their families and friends, sparking a frantic search that soon engulfed the entire town.

After their disappearance, local authorities wasted no time in mobilizing a comprehensive search and rescue operation, deploying trained personnel and canine units to search every inch of the dense forest in a race against time. However, despite their exhausting efforts and relentless determination, Oliver, Max and Ethan's whereabouts remain shrouded in mystery, leaving a trail of unanswered questions and deepening fears.

As the days turned into weeks, the gravity of the situation began to sink in, casting a grim shadow over the once vibrant streets of Everwood. With each passing day, hope waned and despair loomed larger as the community grappled with the harsh reality of unexplained loss plaguing their midst.

Amid the chaos and uncertainty, speculation began to spread, fueling rumors and conjectures about what might have befallen the missing boys. Some speculated about wild beasts lurking in the woods, while others whispered of supernatural forces at play, spinning tales of ancient curses and malevolent spirits haunting the depths of the forest.

But amid the confusion and speculation, one thing remained certain: the Everwood community's unwavering determination to find answers and bring the boy home. From candlelight vigils to fervent prayer gatherings, the city rallied in a show of solidarity and strength, refusing to give in to despair in the face of adversity.

As the investigation into the disappearance of Oliver, Max, and Ethan continues, the Everwood community remains united in its determination to uncover the truth behind this perplexing mystery. With each passing day, the fervent hope of a happy reunion fades, but the bond of love and solidarity that binds the town together remains unbroken, a beacon of hope amidst the darkness that has descended upon their once peaceful home.

Chapter 2: Unraveling Clues

In the picturesque town of Everwood, nestled among towering pines and tranquil lakes, a chilling mystery has unfolded, leaving the tight-knit community in shock and disbelief. It all started one fresh autumn morning when three young boys, known for their adventurous spirit and inseparable bond, disappeared without a trace.

The disappearance sent shockwaves through Everwood, a town where everyone knew everyone else's stuff. As days turned into weeks and weeks into months, the once hopeful search for the missing boys turned into a desperate search for answers. Rumors swirled like autumn leaves in the wind, and speculation abounded among the townspeople.

Despite the efforts of law enforcement and concerned citizens, leads were scarce and the trail seemed to grow colder by the day. Yet amid the uncertainty, a determined group of locals set out to unravel the mystery that has gripped their town.

Mrs. Thompson, the town librarian known for her sharp intellect and insatiable curiosity, has pored over old newspapers and dusty archives in search of any clue that might shed light on the boys' disappearance. Meanwhile, Mr. Jenkins, a retired detective with a keen eye for detail, combed through witness statements and interviewed anyone who might have seen anything unusual that fateful day.

As the investigation progressed, some tantalizing clues began to emerge. A witness reported seeing the boys near an old abandoned mill on the outskirts of town and their laughter echoing through the trees. Another claimed to have seen strange lights flashing in the sky over the lake the night they disappeared.

With each piece of evidence, the puzzle slowly began to take shape. It was clear that the boys had stumbled upon something much more sinister than anyone could have imagined. The townspeople whispered of secret government experiments and alien encounters, while others spoke of ancient curses and supernatural forces at work.

Despite the growing unrest that pervaded the city, the search for the missing boys continued. The volunteers searched every inch of the Everwood, from its dense forests to its murky swamps, refusing to give up hope of one day being reunited with their loved ones.

But just when all hope seemed lost, a breakthrough finally came. A local fisherman discovered a tattered backpack caught in the branches of a tree near a lake, its contents spilling onto the forest floor. Among the scattered items was a crumpled map, its faded ink revealing a hidden trail leading deep into the heart of the wilderness.

With renewed determination, the townspeople followed the map's mysterious clues, each step bringing them closer to the truth. And as they venture deeper into the unknown, they soon uncover a shocking revelation that will change Everwood forever.

The boys appeared to stumble upon a hidden underground bunker hidden beneath the forest floor. Inside, they found evidence of a secret government project that had been conducting experiments on unsuspecting subjects for decades. The boys were unwittingly ensnared in conspiracy and deception, and their disappearance served as a grim reminder of the dangers lurking in the shadows.

When the truth came out, the city of Everwood came together and vowed to never forget the brave boys who sacrificed everything in pursuit of justice. And while their fate remained a mystery, their spirit lived on in the hearts of those who refused to stop searching for the truth.

Ultimately, uncovering clues to the disappearance of the Everwood boys served as a testament to the resilience of the human spirit and the unwavering bond of community in the face of adversity. And while the scars of the past may never fully heal, the people of Everwood vow to never stop looking for answers, no matter where the road may lead.

2.1 The protagonist's determination to find their missing friends.

In the heart of a quaint suburban neighborhood, a group of childhood friends shared a bond forged through years of laughter, adventure, and unbreakable camaraderie. Among them, Jake stood out as a natural leader, and his unwavering determination often saw the group through life's challenges. But when three of their friends mysteriously disappear one fateful summer evening, Jake's resolve is put to the ultimate test.

The disappearance sent shockwaves through the tight-knit community, leaving families distraught and authorities confused. Despite exhaustive search efforts and countless inquiries, the whereabouts of the missing boys remained a haunting mystery. But giving up was never an option for Jake. Fueled by a potent mix of loyalty, guilt, and an unyielding sense of responsibility, he embarks on a relentless quest to uncover the truth and bring his friends home.

As the days turned into weeks and then months, Jake's determination only grew stronger. He searched every inch of their neighborhood, carefully following their steps and examining every detail for clues. Each passing day brought new challenges and setbacks, but Jake refused to despair. His unwavering belief in the power of friendship and the resilience of the human spirit fueled his relentless pursuit.

The journey was full of obstacles, both physical and emotional. Jake faced skepticism and doubt from skeptics who saw his efforts as futile. Still, he was undeterred and channeled his grief and frustration into a single purpose: to find his missing friends and bring them back home to where they belonged.

In his quest for answers, Jake uncovers long-hidden secrets and dark truths lurking beneath the surface of their idyllic community. He delved into the lives of those closest to the missing boys, uncovering hidden agendas and conflicting motives. With each revelation, the line between friend and foe blurred, and Jake found himself navigating a treacherous labyrinth of deception and betrayal.

But amid the chaos and uncertainty, one thing remained steadfast: Jake's unwavering determination to find his friends. He refused to allow fear or doubt to cloud his judgment and moved forward with a determination that bordered on obsession. Each clue, no matter how faint, became a beacon of hope in the darkness, driving him closer and closer to the truth.

As the days stretched into years, Jake's relentless pursuit gained attention far beyond their small community. His story became a symbol of resilience and unwavering loyalty, inspiring others to join the search and rekindling hope in the hearts of those who had lost faith.

And then, when all seemed lost, a breakthrough emerged from the shadows, shedding a glimmer of light on the darkest chapter of their lives. Through sheer perseverance and unwavering determination, Jake uncovers the truth behind his friends' disappearance and unravels the web of lies and deceit that ensnares them all.

In the end, it was Jake's dogged determination that brought his friends back home, reunited them with their families, and restored peace to their shattered community. And while the scars of their ordeal will never fully heal, they served as a testament to the power of friendship and the indomitable spirit of those who refuse to give up, no matter the odds.

2.2 Delving into the boys' backgrounds and possible motivations for vanishing.

In the picturesque town of Everwood, where neighbors know each other by name and children play freely in the streets, a dark cloud hangs over the community after the sudden disappearance of several young boys. As investigators delve into a disturbing mystery, they encounter a complex web of background and potential motivations that could shed light on the mysterious events.

First of all, understanding the background of the missing boys is key to solving the mystery. Each child comes from a unique family dynamic, socioeconomic status, and personal history, all of which can offer clues to their disappearance. Some may have experienced trauma or instability at home, while others may have faced academic or social pressure at school. By piecing together the fragments of their lives, investigators can gain valuable insights into potential vulnerabilities and triggers that may have contributed to their disappearing act.

Furthermore, investigating the motivation behind the boy's disappearance requires a different approach. While some may speculate foul play or kidnapping, it is equally important to consider the internal factors that may have made the boy run away of his own free will. Adolescence is a time of immense emotional turmoil and identity exploration, and it is not uncommon for young individuals to struggle with feelings of alienation, disillusionment, or a desire to escape. Perhaps the boys felt suffocated by the expectations and limitations of their small-town existence, yearning for adventure or autonomy beyond Everwood.

Furthermore, the social dynamics within the peer group cannot be overlooked. Adolescents often navigate complex social hierarchies and power dynamics where bullying, peer pressure, and cliques can have a significant influence on behavior. It is likely that interpersonal conflicts or tensions between the boys may have reached a boiling point and led to drastic actions or decisions driven by a sense of desperation or retribution.

In addition to personal motivations, broader societal influences can also play a role in shaping boys' actions. Everwood Town, like many rural communities, is struggling with its own problems, from economic decline to cultural stagnation. The allure of city life or the promise of a new start elsewhere may have lured boys, offering a glimmer of hope or possibility amidst the familiar surroundings of their hometown.

As investigators sift through evidence and interview witnesses, they must remain vigilant in exploring all possible leads and lines of inquiry. From examining digital traces and surveillance footage to exploring the surrounding wilderness and reaching out to neighboring communities, every effort must be made to uncover the truth behind the disappearance of the Everwood Town boys.

In the heart-wrenching saga of their disappearance, one thing remains abundantly clear: the need for compassion, empathy and an unwavering determination to reach out to their families and the community as a whole. Only by piecing together the complex puzzle of their backgrounds and motivations can we hope to shed light on the dark shadows that loom over Everwood, offering comfort and understanding in the face of uncertainty.

2.3 Discovering cryptic clues and hidden secrets that lead to unexpected revelations.

In the heart of Everwood Town, a picturesque community nestled among towering trees and tranquil streams, a chilling mystery grips the townspeople. Three young boys, vibrant souls full of laughter and innocence, disappeared without a trace. As days turned to weeks and weeks to months, the once tight-knit community was left in shock, haunted by unanswered questions and a sense of foreboding.

Faced with despair, a group of determined locals take on the task of uncovering mysterious clues and hidden secrets that may hold the key to the boys' disappearance. Led by retired detective Mrs. Eleanor Matthews, whose sharp wit and keen eye for detail has earned her a reputation for solving the toughest cases, the team embarks on a journey full of danger and uncertainty.

Their investigation begins in the boys' neighborhood, which is abuzz with whispers of strange happenings and mysterious figures lurking in the shadows. With every knock on the door and every witness they interview, the team uncovers a tangled web of lies and deceit, leading them deeper into the heart of darkness that shrouds the city of Everwood.

But it's not just tangible evidence that drives their search. Drawing on decades of experience, Ms. Matthews teaches her team the art of deciphering mysterious clues hidden in plain sight. From coded messages carved into ancient tree trunks to symbols carved into the walls of long-forgotten buildings, each discovery brings them closer to uncovering the truth.

As days turn to night, the team faces unexpected obstacles and heartbreaking twists. A shadowy figure emerges from the depths of the forest with unclear but undeniably sinister intentions. With danger lurking around every corner, the team must rely on their wits and each other to navigate the treacherous path forward.

But just when all hope seems lost, a breakthrough occurs. A forgotten diary discovered in the attic of an old farmhouse reveals a startling revelation: the boys' disappearance is linked to a decades-old feud that has torn Everwood Town apart. Armed with this newfound knowledge, the team races against time to confront the dark forces that threaten to engulf their beloved community.

In a climactic showdown under a canopy of ancient trees, secrets are revealed and justice is meted out. Battered but resilient, the boys are finally reunited with their families and end the nightmare that has plagued Everwood Town for far too long.

As the sun sets over the horizon, casting a warm glow over the once troubled community, the townspeople gather to celebrate their victory. Although the scars may remain, they stand united and know that in the face of adversity, love and perseverance will always prevail. And as the stars twinkle overhead, a sense of hope and renewal fills the air, reminding them that even in the darkest of times, light always finds a way to shine through.

Chapter 3: The Journey Begins

In the heart of a picturesque village among rolling hills and lush forests, a group of adventurous boys embark on a journey that will change the course of their lives forever. Shrouded in mystery and intrigue, their story captured the townspeople's imagination and resonated for generations. Known for their restless spirits and insatiable curiosity, the boys set out one fateful morning with nothing but a map and a boundless sense of wonder.

As they ventured deeper into the wilderness, their laughter filled the air, mingling with rustling leaves and chirping birds. Each step brought them closer to the unknown and they relished the thrill of exploration. They passed babbling brooks and towering oaks, their eyes bright with the promise of discovery.

But as the sun sank below the horizon and the shadows lengthened, a sense of unease crept over the group. The forest that was once teeming with life grew quiet and foreboding. Whispers of ancient legends and cautionary tales echoed in their minds, but the lure of the unknown beckoned them forward.

Hours turned into days and still the boys pressed on, driven by an unyielding determination to uncover the secrets that lay in the heart of the wilderness. Their supplies were running low and fatigue was gnawing at their bones, but they refused to waver. Their bond grew stronger with each passing moment, forged in the crucible of adversity.

However, as they ventured deeper into the heart of the forest, they came upon a clearing bathed in moonlight, where the trees whispered secrets of long-forgotten times. It was there, amidst the dancing shadows and ethereal glow, that their journey took an unexpected turn.

In the blink of an eye, the boys disappeared without a trace, leaving behind only the echoes of their laughter and the faint smell of adventure. The townspeople were plunged into grief, their hearts heavy with grief and uncertainty. Rumors swirled like autumn leaves in the wind, spinning tales of otherworldly beings and cursed lands.

But amidst the sadness, there remained a glimmer of hope. In the depths of despair, the townspeople have rallied, determined to solve the mystery of the missing boys and bring them home. They searched every inch of the forest and left no stone unturned in their search for answers.

Months turned into years and the fate of the boys still remained a haunting mystery. Yet their spirit lived on in the hearts of those who refused to forget, a testament to the enduring power of friendship and the boundless courage of youth.

And so the journey began again, a timeless tale of adventure and loss woven into the fabric of the village's history. As long as the memory of the missing boys lives on, their legacy will live on, like a beacon of hope in the darkest of nights. And perhaps one day their footsteps will echo again, guiding future generations on their own journey into the unknown.

3.1 Embarking on a perilous journey to follow the trail of the vanished boys.

An eerie silence lingered in the heart of the small, tight-knit community nestled between towering forests and rolling hills. It wasn't just the absence of laughter and playful chatter that unsettled the residents of Willowbrook; it was the inexplicable disappearance of three young boys, the heartbeat of the village, throwing a bow on the once vibrant city.

As dawn broke and the amber hues of the rising sun pierced the dense canopy, murmurs of fear and uncertainty echoed through the cobbled streets. The boys, Oliver, Max, and Ethan, disappeared without a trace, leaving behind a void that seemed impossible to fill. Their disappearance sent shockwaves through Willowbrook, shattering the illusion of safety and tranquility that had cocooned the villagers for generations.

Desperation fueled by grief and fear engulfed the community, forcing them to look for answers where there seemed to be none. With each passing day, the mystery deepened and whispers of sinister forces swirled through the trees like a mist. It is in the midst of this atmosphere of fear and uncertainty that a group of determined individuals, driven by an unrelenting desire for closure, decide to embark on a perilous journey in pursuit of the missing boys.

The search party, led by Jonah, a grizzled woodsman with a weathered face etched with stories of survival and resilience, gathered at the edge of the forest, their resolve tempered by the weight of uncertainty that hung heavy in the air. Armed with lanterns, supplies, and a fierce determination to uncover the truth, they set out into the heart of the wilderness, where shadows danced to the mournful tunes of the wind.

The journey ahead was fraught with peril, as dense undergrowth and treacherous terrain tested their resolve at every turn. Still, fueled by a glimmer of hope that refused to die, they pressed on, each step bringing them closer to the elusive truth that lay shrouded in the depths of the forest.

As they delved deeper into the wilderness, they encountered signs, subtle yet unmistakable, that indicated a presence lurking in the shadows. Strange symbols carved into the bark of ancient trees, whispers carried by the wind, and fleeting flashes of movement in the undergrowth served as breadcrumbs in the labyrinth of uncertainty, leading them ever closer to the core of the mystery.

With each passing moment, the line between reality and myth blurred as tales of ancient souls and forgotten curses whispered through the trees. Still, fueled by a determination forged in the crucible of loss and despair, they refused to waver, and their resolve could not be defied by adversity.

Days turned into nights and nights into weeks, but still they continued, driven by a relentless pursuit of the truth that seemed to elude them at every turn. And then, just as hope was about to fade into oblivion, they came upon a clearing bathed in ethereal moonlight where the silhouettes of three figures stood against the darkness.

They were Oliver, Max, and Ethan, their faces etched with wisdom far beyond their years, their eyes blazing with a fire that spoke of trials overcome and truths revealed. In that fleeting moment, as the veil of mystery lifted, the pieces of the puzzle fell into place, revealing a truth more terrifying than anything they could have imagined.

For the boys did not simply vanish into thin air; they set out on a journey of self-discovery and redemption, guided by forces unseen but undeniably real. And as dawn broke over the horizon, lighting the way ahead with the promise of new beginnings, the people of Willowbrook stood united, their faith in the power of hope and resilience reaffirmed in the face of darkness.

3.2 Facing obstacles and dangers as they venture into unknown territories.

In the picturesque town of Everwood, nestled among lush forests and rolling hills, three young boys have mysteriously disappeared without a trace. Their disappearance sent shockwaves through the community, leaving families gripped by fear and uncertainty. A group of brave individuals, determined to solve the mystery and bring the lost boys home, embark on a perilous journey into the unknown regions surrounding Everwood.

Heading into the uncharted wilderness, the search party faced countless obstacles and dangers lurking in the shadows. Dense undergrowth and tangled vines impeded their progress, forcing them to navigate the treacherous terrain carefully and steadily. Every step forward was met with uncertainty as dense foliage obscured their path and hid unseen threats.

As they delved deeper into the heart of the wilderness, the looming specter of danger became more and more palpable. Wild animals scurried about in the shadows, their eyes glistening with primal hunger. It filled the air with the echoes of the screams of creatures of the night and sent shivers down the spines of the brave souls who dared to tread where others feared to roam. However, despite the looming threat of danger, their determination remained unwavering as they continued their quest to find the missing boys.

In the middle of the harsh landscape, they encountered unexpected challenges that tested their strength and courage. Harsh weather conditions, from sweltering heat to freezing cold, pushed their physical limits to the brink. Torrential rains turned the narrow paths into treacherous rivers and threatened to sweep them away in a deluge of mud and debris. Yet, through sheer determination and unwavering camaraderie, they fought their way forward and were undeterred by the obstacles that stood in their way.

But perhaps the biggest obstacle they faced was the inexorable march of time. With each passing day, hope threatened to die out like the dying embers of a once roaring fire. Yet, in the face of adversity, they clung to the belief that their efforts would not be in vain. Guided by a flickering light of hope, they continued, driven by a single purpose: to bring the lost boys of Everwood back to their loved ones.

Despite the countless challenges they encountered along the way, the search party remained steadfast in their determination. Their unwavering determination and selfless courage served as a beacon of hope in the midst of darkness, inspiring others to join their cause and lend a helping hand.

And then, when all seemed lost, a glimmer of hope broke through the veil of despair. In the tangled undergrowth, they saw a faint trail leading deeper into the wilderness, a trail that held the promise of answers and the possibility of reunion.

With renewed determination they followed the trail into the unknown, their hearts filled with hope and their souls burning with the fervent belief that against all odds they would find the lost boys of Everwood and bring them safely home.

3.3 Forming unlikely alliances and encountering enigmatic figures along the way

In the picturesque town of Everwood, nestled among towering trees and rolling hills, a mysterious disappearance has sent shockwaves through the community. Three boys, loved by all, disappeared without a trace, leaving behind a sense of unease and fear. As the town grapples with this disturbing mystery, an unlikely alliance forms among its residents, united by a shared determination to uncover the truth.

In the heart of the Everwood, where whispers of ancient legends mingle with rustling leaves, a group of individuals from diverse backgrounds unite in meaning. Among them are Sarah, a local librarian with a penchant for solving puzzles, and Jake, a seasoned tracker with an eye for detail. Together they embark on a journey deep into the forest, where secrets are hidden under the canopy.

Their quest leads them to meet mysterious figures shrouded in mystery, each holding a piece of the puzzle they are trying to unravel. From a reclusive hermit who dwells deep in the woods to an eccentric artist whose paintings seem to provide clues to the disappearance of the boys, they encounter an array of characters as varied as the landscape itself.

As they delve deeper into the heart of Everwood, the alliance faces challenges and obstacles at every turn. They navigate treacherous terrain, avoiding lurking dangers and facing their own doubts and fears along the way. Yet with each step forward, she grows stronger in her determination to uncover the truth and bring the missing boys home.

Amidst the towering trees and echoes of the forest's silence, they uncover long-forgotten secrets that shed light on the boys' disappearance. Ancient symbols carved into the bark of trees, cryptic messages hidden in the pages of old books, and whispered tales of a lost civilization emerge as they piece the puzzle together.

But just when they seem to be closing in on the truth, they encounter a formidable adversary, a shadowy figure lurking in the shadows, bent on thwarting their efforts at every turn. Danger is approaching and time is running out, and the alliance must use all its strength and cunning to overcome the obstacles in the way.

In a final showdown beneath the ancient branches of the oldest tree in Everwood, the truth will finally emerge. Lured by the promise of adventure, the boys stumble upon an ancient relic hidden deep in the forest, a relic with the power to grant untold riches to those who possess it. But their greed led them astray and they fell prey to its dark lure.

As the sun sets on Everwood, the town breathes a sigh of relief as the missing boys are reunited with their families. Yet the alliance forged in the face of adversity remains, a testament to the power of unlikely friendships and the resilience of the human spirit in the face of darkness. And among the whispering trees and shifting shadows, the legend of the Everwood lives on, a reminder of the mysteries that lie just beyond our understanding.

Chapter 4: The Truth Revealed

In the picturesque town of Everwood, nestled among tranquil forests and rolling hills, a sinister mystery has unfolded, gripping the community in fear and uncertainty. Three young boys; Oliver, Max, and Ethan, disappear without a trace, sending shockwaves through the tight-knit community. As days turned to weeks and weeks to months, speculation swirled and rumors spread like wildfire, shrouding the truth in a shroud of mystery.

The disappearance of Oliver, Max, and Ethan initially baffled the authorities and residents. The boys were known for their adventurous spirit, often exploring the vast wilderness surrounding Everwood. However, as the days dragged on in the agonizing search, hope began to fade and an eerie silence haunted the once picturesque town.

Despite the exhaustive efforts of law enforcement and volunteers, the boys seemed to vanish into thin air. Every trail went cold and every trail led to a dead end. The community grappled with unanswered questions and lingering fear, wondering what could have happened to the beloved trio.

Amidst the uncertainty, whispers of conspiracy and foul play began to emerge. Some speculated that the boys had stumbled upon something they weren't meant to see, a secret hidden deep in the heart of Everwood. Others whispered of supernatural powers at play and spun tales of mythical creatures lurking in the shadows of the forest.

As the investigation dragged on, tensions grew and trust in the once tight-knit community began to grow. Families held their children close, fearing that they too might fall prey to whatever unseen danger lurked in the shadows.

However, just when it seemed all hope was lost, there was a breakthrough that illuminated the darkest corners of Everwood. A local historian dedicated to uncovering the city's hidden secrets has come across a long-forgotten diary hidden in the archives.

Written by a former resident of Everwood, the journal detailed a series of events that bore a striking resemblance to the disappearances of Oliver, Max, and Ethan. According to the paper, decades ago three young boys disappeared under eerily similar circumstances, leaving behind a trail of unanswered questions and lingering fear.

Armed with this newfound information, the investigators delve deeper into Everwood's dark history, uncovering long-buried secrets and hidden truths. What they discovered sent shockwaves through the community and changed the perception of their idyllic town forever.

Everwood is revealed to be harboring a dark secret, a secret that has been carefully hidden for generations. Beneath its picturesque facade lay a tangled web of deceit, betrayal and unspeakable horrors. The disappearance of Oliver, Max, and Ethan was not an isolated incident, but rather a symptom of a much larger problem that has plagued Everwood for decades.

When the truth came out, the community faced the harsh reality of their town's dark past. Yet amid the despair, there was also a glimmer of hope, hope that when they faced the truth, the wounds that had long festered beneath the surface could begin to heal.

After the reveal, the disappearance of Oliver, Max, and Ethan served as a catalyst for change in Everwood. The community came together, determined to break free from the shackles of their city's troubled history and forge a new path forward. Although the fates of Oliver, Max and Ethan remain unknown, their legacy lives on as a reminder of the resilience of the human spirit and the strength of community in the face of adversity. And as the sun set over the rolling hills of Everwood, casting long shadows over its storied past, the city stood united, ready to write a new chapter in its history, a chapter defined not by darkness and despair, but by hope, healing, and Redemption.

4.1 Confronting the dark truth behind the boys' disappearance

In the peaceful town of Everwood, nestled among dense forests and rolling hills, a sinister mystery has gripped the community for years. It began with the sudden disappearance of three young boys, whose fate remained shrouded in darkness and cast a long shadow over the city.

As days turned to weeks and weeks to months, hope dwindled and fear took root in the hearts of the people of Everwood. The once peaceful streets echoed with whispers of speculation and suspicion as everyone grappled with the unanswered questions that haunted their minds. What happened to the boys? Who was responsible? And why did it happen in their idyllic town?

Despite an exhaustive search and countless leads, the boys' whereabouts have remained elusive, leaving their families divided by grief and uncertainty. Each passing year only deepened the wounds, as birthdays were not celebrated and holidays became a painful reminder of their absence.

But beneath the surface of Everwood's picturesque facade, secrets spilled like untended wounds. Whispers began to surface about a secret group lurking in the shadows, preying on the innocence of the city's youth. Rumors of dark rituals and sacrificial rituals sent chills down the spines of those brave enough to entertain such dark thoughts.

As the community grappled with the troubling revelations, a sense of urgency flooded Everwood. They could no longer turn a blind eye to the darkness lurking in their midst. The time has come to face the truth, no matter how painful it may be.

With renewed determination, a dedicated team of investigators dove into the heart of the mystery, following every lead and unraveling every thread in their quest for justice. Their tireless efforts uncovered a web of deceit and betrayal that ran far deeper than anyone could have imagined.

Through careful investigation and unwavering persistence, the truth began to emerge, bit by bit agonizing. The disappearance of the boys was not the result of random chance or chance, but a carefully orchestrated plan driven by greed and malice.

It was a revelation that shook Everwood to its foundations and forced the community to confront the darkest aspects of human nature lurking in their own backyard. But when the truth was finally revealed, there came a glimmer of hope, a chance for healing and closure for those left behind.

As the sun set over the quiet town of Everwood, casting long shadows across the landscape, a sense of determination settled over the community. While the scars would undoubtedly remain, they could take solace in the knowledge that justice had been served and the memory of the three boys would live on, a testament to the resilience of the human spirit in the face of unimaginable darkness.

4.2 Unravelling a conspiracy that shakes the foundations of their community.

In the peaceful enclave of Everwood Town, nestled among towering pines and whispering winds, beneath the idyllic surface lurked a disturbing secret that threatened to shatter the tranquility of its residents. It began with the inexplicable disappearance of three boys, their laughter and footsteps disappearing into the depths of the forest, leaving only a void of unanswered questions and lingering fear.

As days turned into weeks and weeks into months, the once tight-knit community found itself engulfed in a maelstrom of speculation and paranoia. Whispers echoed through the streets, each carrying a different story of what had befallen the missing trio. Some spoke of wild beasts lurking in the shadows, others of a mysterious figure haunting the woods. Amidst the cacophony of theories, however, one disturbing notion has taken root, that something far more sinister is at play, something woven into the very fabric of Everwood Town itself.

It was in this atmosphere of uncertainty that a small group of determined individuals emerged, driven by an insatiable desire for truth and justice. Delving into the darkest corners of the city, they uncovered secrets that had long been hidden under layers of deception and denial. As they pieced together the scraps of information, a chilling revelation began to emerge, the boys' disappearance was not a random act of fate, but a carefully orchestrated plan, created by unseen hands with nefarious intent.

Suspicion soon turned towards the powerful, their influence casting a long shadow over the city.

Rumors of corruption and conspiracy spread like wildfire, igniting a storm of outrage and indignation. Yet with each step forward, the truth seemed to slip further from their grasp, shrouded in a veil of lies and deceit.

Amid the chaos and despair, however, there was a glimmer of hope - a breakthrough in the form of a long-forgotten diary, hidden in the attic of an old abandoned house. Its pages whispered of dark rites and ancient rituals that hinted at a connection between the missing boys and a secret society that had long dwelt in the shadows of the city of Everwood.

Armed with their newfound knowledge, the group pressed on, their determination unwavering in the face of adversity. With each revelation, they got closer to the core of the conspiracy, uncovering a web of deception that stretched far beyond their wildest imaginations. And when the truth finally came out, the foundations of their community shook, shaken to their core by the knowledge that evil lurked not only in the depths of the forest, but in the hearts of those they once trusted.

Yet amidst the darkness, there remained a glimmer of hope, the promise of redemption and renewal as the people of Everwood Town came together, united in their determination to face the shadows of their past and forge a brighter future from the ashes of deceit. . For in the end it was not the darkness that defined them, but the light of courage and perseverance that saw them through the darkest of nights.

4.3 Resolving to bring justice to those responsible and to find closure for the families left behind.

In the quiet, peaceful enclave of Everwood Town, nestled among the lush green surroundings, a shadow looms over the community, the unsolved disappearance of three young boys. What started as an ordinary day of discovery and adventure for these young people turned into a nightmare for their families and the entire town. The mysterious circumstances surrounding their disappearing act have left gaping wounds in the hearts of those close to them, and the pursuit of justice has become a relentless pursuit, fueled by a collective determination to bring closure to those left behind.

Known for their inseparable bond and insatiable curiosity, three boys embark on a seemingly innocent journey deep into the green wilderness of Everwood. It was familiar terrain that they had passed countless times before, but on that fateful day, fate seemed to have a different plan for them. As the hours turned into days and the days into weeks, the once hopeful search and rescue efforts gradually gave way to the grim acceptance of the harsh reality that the boys had disappeared without a trace.

However, in the midst of despair and anguish, the community of Everwood refused to succumb to the darkness that threatened to consume them. Instead, they come together and form a tight-knit support network dedicated to uncovering the truth behind the unexplained disappearance. From conducting extensive search missions across the vast forests of Everwood to utilizing the expertise of seasoned investigators, no stone is left unturned in the relentless pursuit of justice.

For the families of the missing boys, each passing day without answers only deepened the wounds of uncertainty and grief. Yet, in the face of unimaginable adversity, they found solace in the unwavering support of their neighbors and the tireless efforts of law enforcement, determined to bring their loved ones home, no matter the cost.

As the investigation into the disappearance of the three boys intensified, whispers of suspicion and conspiracy began to spread within the tight-knit community of

Everwood. Rumors of secret meetings and hidden agendas cast a shadow of doubt over the once-idyllic city and threatened to tear apart the very fabric of trust that had bound its residents together for generations.

But amid the chaos and uncertainty, one thing remained steadfast, a collective determination to seek justice for the three boys and find closure for their grieving families. It was a promise etched into the hearts of every resident of Everwood, a solemn oath that he would never rest until the truth was revealed and those responsible for their actions were brought to justice.

As days turned to months and months to years, the determination of the Everwood community never wavered. While the passage of time may have clouded memories for some, for the families of the missing boys, the pain and longing remain as raw as ever. Yet in their darkest moments, they found strength in the unwavering support of their neighbors and the unyielding determination of those determined to see justice done.

In the heart of Everwood Town, amid towering trees and whispered secrets, the search for justice continues, a beacon of hope shining brightly in the darkness, guiding the way forward as the community stands united in its determination to close the chapter of sadness and uncertainty that has haunted them for far too long.

Conclusion

The disappearance of Oliver, Max and Ethan in the city of Everwood is a confusing and tragic story that has left the community in a state of shock and confusion. As the investigation unfolds, various theories and speculations have emerged, but the ultimate fate of the three boys remains unknown. This mysterious incident not only cast a shadow over Everwood, but also sparked debate and raised questions about the safety and security of small towns and the vulnerability of their residents.

At the heart of this narrative is the deep sense of loss experienced by the families, friends and neighbors of Oliver, Max and Ethan. Their sudden disappearance shattered the peace of Everwood and left behind a void that seems impossible to fill. The once vibrant streets now echo with an eerie silence, serving as a constant reminder of the three young lives taken so suddenly.

The community's response to the disappearance was one of unity and solidarity, with residents coming together to support each other in their time of need. Candlelight vigils, search drives and community gatherings have become commonplace as the city grapples with an overwhelming sense of grief and uncertainty. In the face of adversity, the people of Everwood have shown resilience and compassion, refusing to give in to despair despite the bleak circumstances.

As the investigation into the disappearance unfolds, authorities have faced many challenges and obstacles. Despite their tireless efforts, the trail seems to grow colder with each passing day, leaving investigators grasping at straws in their search for answers. The lack of concrete evidence and clues only fueled speculation and fueled rumors, further complicating the already complex puzzle surrounding the boys' disappearance.

In the absence of definitive answers, various theories and conjectures have emerged, each offering insight into the possible fate of Oliver, Max, and Ethan. Some believe that the boys may have simply gotten lost in the dense forest surrounding the Everwood, while others speculate that foul play was involved. As time passes, the line between fact and fiction blurs more and more, leaving the truth shrouded in uncertainty.

The media frenzy surrounding the case only increased the pressure on both the authorities and the community, and reporters flocked to Everwood looking for the next headline. Rumors and misinformation are spreading like an avalanche, further complicating an already complex situation. In the age of social media, the story of the missing boys caught the attention of people far beyond Everwood, turning their tragedy into a spectacle for the masses.

Yet amidst the chaos and uncertainty, there are still moments of hope and resilience. The families' unwavering determination to find their missing loved ones serves as a beacon of light in the darkness and inspires others to never give up hope. Acts of kindness and solidarity abound as the community comes together to seek closure and refuses to be consumed by fear and despair.

As days turn into weeks and weeks into months, the search for Oliver, Max and Ethan continues. Although the road ahead may be long and full of challenges, the people of Everwood remain steadfast in their determination to bring the boy home. For in the face of tragedy, it is the strength of the human spirit that shines brightest and illuminates even the darkest nights. And so the story of three boys who disappeared in the town of Everwood serves as a poignant reminder of the fragility of life and the enduring power of hope.